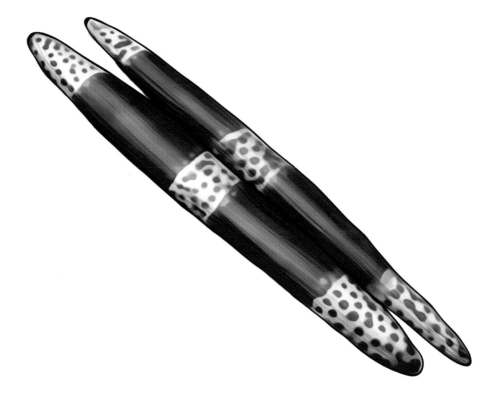

1

© Knowledge Books and Software

Music was part of the First Peoples' lives. Music was for singing, dancing and ceremonies.

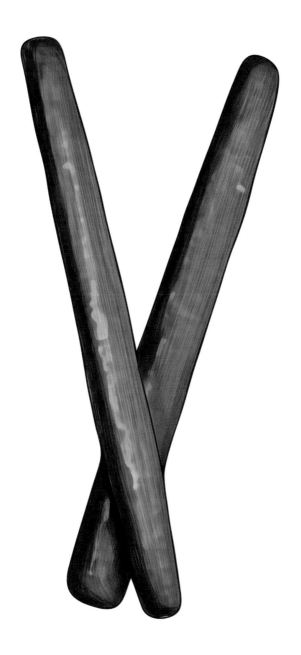

Music was made by a 'didg-er-i-doo'. The sound was made by blowing air through the pipe.

5

This is a bullroarer. It makes a very low sound. It is for a secret ceremony. It can make special sounds for the First Peoples.

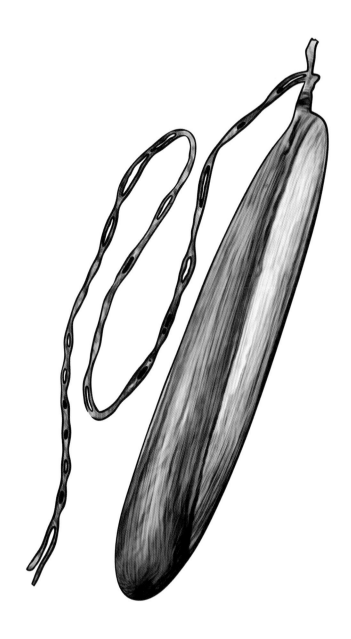

First People would use music in special ceremonies. These ceremonies are secret. Music and dance form part of the ceremony.

These men did a dance with music and special body marks. This was a corroboree.

11

The dance could be for a special animal. The spirit of the animal helps the dancer.

Each tribe had special dance and music. These dances were for spirits.

15

The tribes had different costumes and marks. The First Peoples had many ways of dance.

17

Special body paint was done.
These are decorations and
marks. This was a special dance
of the people.

19

The corroboree was part of the
First Peoples' dance and music.

21

Dancing spirits were painted on the walls of caves.

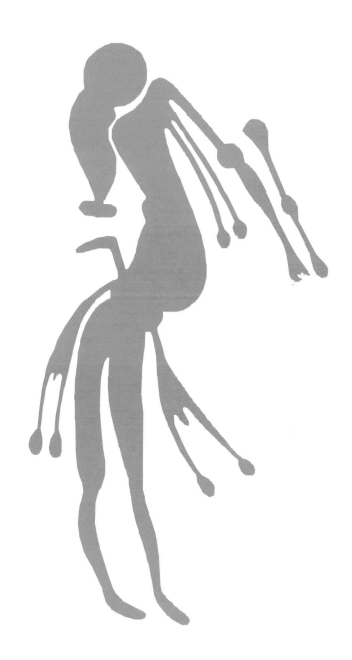

23

Word bank

dance

music

singing

ceremony

didgeridoo

blowing

through

bullroarer

secret

cooroboree

spirit

animal

costumes

decoration